To

_____

From

Nicole Saarah-Mensah ☺

2020 Forever ♡

365 DAY
BRIGHTENERS™

to Lift Your Spirits

365 Day Brighteners™ to Lift Your Spirits

Copyright © 2004 DaySpring® Cards, Inc.
Published by Garborg's®, a brand of DaySpring® Cards, Inc.
Siloam Springs, Arkansas
www.dayspring.com

Scripture quotations are from the following sources: The HOLY BIBLE, NEW INTERNATIONAL VERSION® (NIV)® © 1973, 1978, 1984 by International Bible Society. Used by permission of Zondervan Publishing House. The Living Bible (TLB) © 1971 by permission of Tyndale House Publishers, Inc., Wheaton, IL. THE MESSAGE © 1993, 1994, 1995, 1996. Used by permission of NavPress Publishing Group.

ISBN 1-58061-786-7

Printed in China

365 DAY BRIGHTENERS™

to Lift Your Spirits

GARBORG'S®

because every day is a gift

First things first!
But not necessarily in that order.

JANUARY 1

A boy, frustrated with all the rules he had to follow, asked his father, "Dad, when will I be old enough to do as I please?" The father answered immediately, "I don't know, son. Nobody has lived that long yet."

JANUARY 2

Newspaper Ad:
Open House at Body Shapers Toning Salon—
Free coffee and donuts.

JANUARY 3

The sooner you fall behind, the more time you'll have to catch up.

Careful planning puts you ahead in the long run;
hurry and scurry puts you further behind.

PROVERBS 21.5 THE MESSAGE

JANUARY 4

Christmas Break was over and the teacher was asking the class about their vacations.

"We visited our family in Punxsutawney, Pennsylvania," Michael replied.

"Those sound like excellent vocabulary words," the teacher said. "Can you tell the class how you spell that?"

Michael thought about it and said, "You know, come to think of it, we went to Ohio."

JANUARY 5

A mother asked her children just before
entering a church service, "And why
is it necessary to be quiet in church?"
Annie replied, "Because people are sleeping."

JANUARY 6

Church blooper: During the absence of our pastor, we enjoyed the rare privilege of hearing a good sermon from a great minister.

JANUARY 7

One day I was reading a newspaper.
On page two was a picture of a famous politician
and his gorgeous wife. Slightly jealous of the
politician, I turned to my wife and said,
"It's unfair that the biggest jerks in the world
catch the most beautiful wives."
My wife smiled and replied,
"Why, thank you dear."

JANUARY 8

All of us could take a lesson from the weather.
It pays no attention to criticism.

JANUARY 9

Most plans are just inaccurate predictions.

BEN BAYOL

We humans keep brainstorming options and plans,
but God's purpose prevails.

PROVERBS 19:21 THE MESSAGE

JANUARY 10

The newly wed wife said to her husband when he returned from work: "I have great news for you. Pretty soon we're going to be three in this house instead of two."
The husband started glowing with happiness and kissing his wife said: "Oh darling, I'm the happiest man in the world."
But then she said: "I'm glad that you feel that way since Mom will be here in the morning!"

JANUARY 11

Those bellhops in Miami are tip happy.
I ordered a deck of playing cards and the bellboy
made fifty-two trips to my room.

Henny Youngman

January 12

Be careful of your thoughts; they may become words at any moment.

IRA GASSEN

JANUARY 13

A rookie cop was asked the following question on an examination: "How would you go about dispersing a crowd?" He answered: "Take up an offering. That does it every time."

Incompetence. When you earnestly
believe you can make up for
a lack of skill by doubling your effort,
there's no end to what you can't do.

JANUARY 15

There are some friends you know
you will have for the rest of your life. You're
welded together by love, trust, respect,
loss—or simple embarrassment.

A true friend sticks by you like family.

PROVERBS 18:24 THE MESSAGE

JANUARY 16

A minister told his congregation, "Next week I plan to preach about the sin of lying. To help you understand my sermon, I would like you all to read the seventeenth chapter of Mark." The following Sunday, the minister asked for a show of hands. He wanted to know how many people had read Mark 17. Every hand went up. The minister smiled and said, "Before I begin my sermon about the sin of lying, I would like to remind everyone that Mark only has sixteen chapters."

JANUARY 17

T here are moments when everything goes well, but don't be frightened, it won't last.

JULES RENARD

JANUARY 18

A heavy snowstorm closed the schools in one town. When the children returned to school a few days later, one grade school teacher asked her students whether they had used the time away from school constructively. "I sure did, teacher," one little girl replied. "I just prayed for more snow."

JANUARY 19

Time between slipping on a peel
and smacking the pavement: 1 bananosecond.

JANUARY 20

After she woke up, a woman told her husband,
"I just dreamed that you gave me a pearl
necklace for our anniversary. What do you
think it means?"
"You'll know tonight." he said.
That evening, the man came home with
a small package and gave it to his wife. Delighted,
she opened it to find a book entitled
"The Meaning of Dreams."

JANUARY 21

Lord, make my words soft and tender,
for tomorrow I may have to eat them.

*Pleasant words are a honeycomb,
sweet to the soul and healing.*

PROVERBS 16:24 NIV

JANUARY 22

I took up meditation. I like to have an espresso first just to make it more challenging.

BETSY SALKIND

JANUARY 23

There are people who make things happen,
those who watch what happens, and those
who wonder what happened.

JANUARY 24

$\mathbb{A}$ mother was teaching her 3-year-old the Lord's prayer. For several evenings at bedtime she repeated it after her mother. One night she said she was ready to solo. The mother listened with pride as she carefully enunciated each word, right up to the end of the prayer. "Lead us not into temptation," she prayed, "but deliver us some E-mail, Amen."

JANUARY 25

I bet that Van Gogh guy cut off his ear by accident and made up that 'lost love' story so he wouldn't look stupid.

ANDY PIERSON

JANUARY 26

Dentist to Patient: "Would you help me out? I'd like you to give a few of your loudest screams?"

Patient: "Why, Doc? I didn't feel a thing!"

Dentist: "I know, but there are so many people in the waiting room right now and I don't want to miss the five o'clock football game."

JANUARY 27

$\int$ ign posted in a cafeteria, "Shoes are required to eat in the cafeteria. Socks can eat any place they want."

So eat your meals heartily, not worrying about what others say about you.

1 CORINTHIANS 10:30 THE MESSAGE

JANUARY 28

My friend's preparations for a visit from
her children included a trip to the bank.
Waiting in line at the teller's window, she
lamented to the middle-aged man behind her,
"My children are in their 20s, and I'm still
giving them money. When does it end?"
"I'm not sure I'm the one to ask,"
the man said while glancing uncomfortably
at a paper in his hand, "I'm here
to deposit a check from my mother."

JANUARY 29

My father taught me how to swim when I was five years old. He took me down to the river and threw me in. I wouldn't have minded, but people were ice-skating at the time.

BOB PHILLIPS

JANUARY 30

I used to have an open mind
but my brains kept falling out.

All music is folk music. I ain't never heard no horse sing a song.

LOUIS ARMSTRONG

FEBRUARY 1

I poured Spot remover on my dog.
Now he's gone.

FEBRUARY 2

Never argue with an idiot. They drag
you down to their level.

*Because of you I look like an idiot, I walk
around ashamed to show my face.*

FEBRUARY 3

I always try to go the extra mile at work,
but my boss always finds me and brings me back.

FEBRUARY 4

A man was telling his neighbor, "I just bought a new hearing aid. It cost me four thousand dollars, but it's state of the art."

"Really," answered the neighbor.

"What kind is it?"

"Twelve thirty."

FEBRUARY 5

If it were not for Thomas Edison, we would all be watching television in the dark.

FEBRUARY 6

I can please only one person per day.
Today is not your day.
Tomorrow isn't looking so good either.

FEBRUARY 7

There was a man driving down the road behind an 18 wheeler, at every stoplight the trucker would get out of the cab, run back and bang on the trailer door. After seeing this at several intersections in a row the motorist followed him until he pulled into a parking lot. When they both had come to a stop, the truck driver once again jumped out and started banging on the trailer door. The motorist went up to him and said, "I don't mean to be nosey but why do you keep banging on that door?" To which the trucker replied, "Sorry, can't talk now, I have 20 tons of canaries and a 10 ton limit, so I have to keep half of them flying at all times."

FEBRUARY 8

If things get any worse, I'll have to ask you to stop helping me.

Give us help for the hard task;
human help is worthless.

PSALM 60:11 THE MESSAGE

FEBRUARY 9

I went to an authentic Mexican restaurant.
The waiter poured the water and then
warned me not to drink it.

BRAD GARRETT

FEBRUARY 10

Church blooper: Low Self-esteem
Support Group will meet Thursday,
from 7 to 8:30 P.M. Please use the back door.

FEBRUARY 11

By working faithfully eight hours a day, you may eventually get to be boss and work twelve.

ROBERT FROST

FEBRUARY 12

I don't think I'll ever have a mother's intuition.
My sister left me alone in a restaurant
with my 12-month-old nephew.
I said, "What do I do if he cries?"
She said, "Give him some vegetables."
It turns out that jalapenos are not his favorite.

FEBRUARY 13

Research tells us that fourteen out
of any ten individuals like chocolate.

SANDRA BOYNTON

FEBRUARY 14

The other night, my wife and I were going out for dinner. She put on eyebrow pencil, eye shadow, eyeliner, mascara, toner, blush and lipstick, then turned to me and said, "Does this look natural?"

Charm can be deceptive and beauty doesn't last.

PROVERBS 31:30 TLB

FEBRUARY 15

The teacher wrote "Like I ain't had no fun in months" on the board and said, "Timmy, how should I correct that?"
Timmy replied, "Maybe get a new boyfriend?"

FEBRUARY 16

You may be only one person in the world, but you may also be the world to one person.

FEBRUARY 17

During dinner at a local restaurant,
I called the waitress over and said,
"Ma'am, this baked potato is bad."
She nodded, picked up the potato and smacked
it. Then she put it back on my plate and said,
"Sir, if that potato causes any more trouble,
you just let me know."

FEBRUARY 18

I don't have an attitude problem.
You have a perception problem.

FEBRUARY 19

If the shoe fits...buy it in every color.

FEBRUARY 20

${O}$h Lord, help me to keep my big mouth shut
until I know what I'm talking about.

The right word at the right time—beautiful!

PROVERBS 15:23 THE MESSGE

FEBRUARY 21

In a courtroom, a purse-snatcher is on trial
and the victim is stating what happened.
She says, "Yes, that is him. I saw him clear as day.
I'd remember his face anywhere."
At which point, the defendant bursts out, "You
couldn't see my face, lady. I was wearing a mask!"

FEBRUARY 22

Bills travel through the mail
at twice the speed of checks.

FEBRUARY '23

Lord, so far today I've not been grumpy, selfish, greedy, envious, proud, or angry. I'm really pleased about that. But in a few minutes now I'm going to get up, and from then on, I'll probably need a lot more help.

FEBRUARY 24

Dogs have owners.
Cats have staff.

February 25

Junk is something you've kept for years and throw away three weeks before you need it.

FEBRUARY 26

The balding middle-aged man asked his barber, "Why charge me the full price for cutting my hair—there's so little of it."
"Well," said the barber, "actually I don't charge for cutting it. What you're paying for is my searching for it!"

When a man has lost his hair and is bald, he is clean.

LEVITICUS 13:40 NIV

FEBRUARY 27

How long a minute is depends on what side of the bathroom door you're on.

FEBRUARY 28

A co-worker asked if I knew what to do about a computer problem that was preventing her from getting E-mail. After calling the help desk, I told my colleague that E-mail was being delayed to check for a computer virus. "It's a variant of the *I Love You* virus, only worse." "What could be worse?" my single co-worker asked wryly. *"The Let's Just Be Friends virus?"*

FEBRUARY 29

The main purpose of holding children's
parties is to remind yourself that there
are children more awful than your own.

MARCH 1

There was an unexpected knock on my door, and I opened the peephole and asked, "Who's there?"
"Parcel post, ma'am. I have a package that needs a signature."
"Where's the package?" I asked suspiciously. The deliveryman held it up.
"Could I see some ID?" I said, still not convinced.
"Lady," he replied wearily, "if I wanted to break into your house, I'd probably just use these." And he pulled out the keys I had left in the door.

MARCH 2

I am not an organ donor, but I once gave an old piano to the Salvation Army.

MARCH 3

$\int$uccess is relative—the more success,
the more relatives.

He blessed them and told them to share their
great wealth with their relatives back home.

JOSHUA 22:8 TLB

MARCH 4

A first-year astronomy student was heard saying, "Oh, I can see how astronomers figure out the distance of the stars and their size and temperatures and all that. What really gets me is how they find out what their names are!"

MARCH 5

Here at First National, you're not
just a number—you're two numbers,
a dash, three more numbers, another dash,
and another number.

MARCH 6

My therapist told me the way to achieve true inner peace is to finish what I start. So far today I have finished a cheese pizza and 2 bags of chips. I feel better already.

MARCH 7

A teen-aged boy with spiked hair, nose ring and baggy clothes was overheard telling a friend, "I don't really like to dress like this, but it keeps my parents from dragging me everywhere with them."

MARCH 8

My first day in basic training, we were lined up in a row, each of us in turn having to shout our last names. After the guy next to me had yelled, "Florence," it was my turn. I had no sooner called out my name than the training instructor was in my face, demanding to know if I was some kind of smart aleck. Satisfied that I wasn't, the red-faced instructor told me never to stand next to Florence again.

CHARLES W. NIGHTINGALE

MARCH 9

I asked for strength and God gave me difficulties to make me strong. I think maybe next time I'll just be content being weak!

That is why, for Christ's sake, I delight in weaknesses, in insults, in hardships, in persecutions, in difficulties.

2 CORINTHIANS 12:10 NIV

MARCH 10

A teacher was winding up a discussion in her fourth grade class on the importance of curiosity. "Where would we be today if no one had ever been curious?" One of her students piped in, "In the Garden of Eden?"

MARCH 11

Ratio of an igloo's circumference
to its diameter: Eskimo Pi.

MARCH 12

When my mother was called for jury duty, she felt confident of her ability to answer the questions asked of prospective jurors. Since I am an attorney, I had filled her in on what to expect. Asked about the occupations of family members, Mom answered, "My son is a lawyer." As a follow-up, she was asked if she had ever used the services of an attorney.

"Only to mow my lawn," she said.

MARCH 13

Close to 7/5ths of all people
do not understand fractions.

MARCH 14

I was invited to an old friends' home for dinner one evening. My friend preceded every request to his wife with endearing terms—Honey, My Love, Darling, Sweetheart, Pumpkin, etc. They had been married almost 50 years and, clearly, were still very much in love. While the wife was in the kitchen, I leaned over and told my friend, "I think it's wonderful that, after all these years, you still call your wife those loving pet names." The old man hung his head. "Well to tell the truth," he said, "I forgot her name about 10 years ago."

MARCH 15

If you cannot convince them, confuse them.

HARRY S. TRUMAN

Everything was in confusion. In fact, most of them didn't even know why they were there.

ACTS 19.32 TLB

MARCH 16

2,000 pounds of Chinese soup:
Won ton.

MARCH 17

A man is laying on the operating table, about to be operated on by his son, the surgeon. The father says, "Son, take good care of me. Remember...if anything happens to me, your mother is coming to live with you."

MARCH 18

You know the speed of light,
so what's the speed of dark?

MARCH 19

The boss called one of his employees into the office. "Rob," he said, "you've been with the company for a year. You started off in the mailroom, one week later you were promoted to a sales position, and one month after that you were promoted to district manager of the sales department. Just four short months later, you were promoted to vice-chairman. Now it's time for me to retire, and I want you to take over the company. What do you say to that?"

"Thanks," said the employee.

"Thanks?" the boss replied. "Is that all you can say?"

"Uuuhhh...thanks, Dad?"

MARCH 20

If you can't see the bright side of life,
polish the dull side.

MARCH 21

Church blooper: The church will host
an evening of fine dining, superb
entertainment, and gracious hostility.

*Take from my hand this cup filled
to the brim with my anger.*

JEREMIAH 25:15 NLT

MARCH 22

A husband and wife were involved in a petty argument, both of them unwilling to admit they might be in error. "I'll admit I'm wrong," the wife told her husband in a conciliatory attempt, "if you'll admit I'm right."
He agreed and, like a gentleman, insisted she go first. "I'm wrong," she said. With a twinkle in his eye, he responded, "You're right!"

MARCH 23

I am reading a most interesting book about anti-gravity. I just can't put it down.

MARCH 24

It was the end of the day when I parked my police van in front of the station. As I gathered my equipment, my K-9 partner, Jake, was barking, and I saw a little boy staring in at me. "Is that a dog you got back there?" he asked. "It sure is," I replied. Puzzled, the boy looked at me and then towards the back of the van. Finally he said, "What'd he do?"

MARCH 25

The chance of the bread falling with the buttered side down is directly proportional to the cost of the carpet.

MARCH 26

How is it one careless match can start a forest fire, but it takes a whole box to start a campfire?

MARCH 27

It may be that your sole purpose in life
is simply to serve as a warning to others.

God hath chosen the foolish things
of the world to confound the wise.

1 CORINTHIANS 1:27 KJV

MARCH 28

$\mathbb{A}$ man learned shortly before quitting time that he had to attend a meeting. He tried unsuccessfully to locate his car-pool members to let them know that he would not be leaving with them. Hastily he scribbled a message to one fellow and left it on his desk: "I have a last-minute meeting. Leave without me. Dave." At 7:00 P.M., the man stopped at his desk and found this note: "Meet us at the bar and grill across the street. You drove, you idiot."

MARCH 29

I'm not 40-something.
I'm $39.95, plus shipping and handling.

MARCH 30

Why can't women put on mascara
with their mouths closed?

MARCH 31

The wife heard her husband come home much earlier than his usual time. She said, "Hon, what happened to your lodge meeting?" "It was postponed," he replied. "The wife of the Grand Exalted Potentate wouldn't let him attend tonight."

APRIL 1

Never argue with a fool. People
might not know the difference!

APRIL 2

W

hen you have exhausted all possibilities,
remember this—you haven't.

THOMAS EDISON

*I know your deeds, your love and faith,
your service and perseverance, and that you
are now doing more than you did at first.*

REVELATIONS 2:19 NIV

APRIL 3

"An abstract noun," the teacher said,
"is something you can think of,
but you can't touch. Can anyone
give me an example of one?"
"Sure," a teenage boy replied.
"How about my dad's new car."

APRIL 4

W

hen you're right, no one remembers.
When you're wrong, no one forgets.

APRIL 5

If a messy kitchen is a happy kitchen,
then this kitchen is delirious.

APRIL 6

A lady lost her handbag during a day
of shopping. It was found by an honest little
boy and returned to her. Looking in her purse,
she commented, "Hmmm.... That's funny.
When I lost my bag there was a $20 bill in it.
Now there are twenty singles."
The boy quickly replied, "That's right, lady.
The last time I found a lady's purse,
she didn't have change for a reward."

APRIL 7

γou may touch the dust in this house, but please don't write in it! If you do write in the dust, please don't put a date on it!

APRIL 8

$\int$mart is when you believe only half
of what you hear. Brilliant is when
you know which half to believe.

ORBEN'S CURRENT COMEDY

*You don't have to be a genius to understand these
things, just use your common sense.*

LUKE 12:57 THE MESSAGE

APRIL 9

I live in a semi-rural area. We recently had a new neighbor call the local township administrative office to request the removal of the Deer Crossing sign on our road. The reason: Too many deer were being hit by cars and he didn't want them to cross there anymore.

APRIL 10

Always remember that you are absolutely
unique. Just like everyone else.

APRIL 11

One day a guy on a vacation
heard of an American Indian with
an amazing memory, so he decided to visit
the guy and see what the big deal was.
He went to the Indian and asked him,
"What did you eat for breakfast on July 2, 1961?"
The Indian replied, "Eggs."
The same man came back 10 years later to see
the Indian again. He greeted him by saying, "How."
The Indian said, "Fried."

APRIL 12

When all is lost,
ask the I.R.S.—they'll find something.

DOUG HORTON

APRIL 13

Everyone has a photographic memory.
Some just don't have film.

APRIL 14

$\int$ mith: I hate paying my tax bill.
Brown: You should pay up with a smile.
Smith: I've offered them a smile,
but they insist on money.

BOB PHILLIPS

*Give everyone what you owe him: If you owe taxes,
pay taxes; if revenue, then revenue; if respect, then
respect; if honor, then honor.*

ROMANS 13:7 NIV

APRIL 15

A friend is someone who thinks you're
a good egg even though you're slightly cracked.

APRIL 16

Over breakfast, a woman said to her husband,
"I bet you don't know what day this is."
"Of course I do," he indignantly answered.
"How could you think I would forget?"
He left for work. A few hours later the doorbell
rang. When the woman opened the door, she
was handed a dozen long-stemmed red roses.
In the afternoon, a two pound box of her favorite
chocolates arrived. Later, a designer dress
was delivered. The woman couldn't wait
for her husband to come home.
"First the flowers, then the chocolate, and then
the dress!" she exclaimed. "I've never had a more
wonderful Arbor Day in all my life!"

APRIL 17

Late one night in the Washington, D.C. area
a mugger wearing a ski mask jumped
into the path of a well-dressed man
and stuck a gun in his ribs.
"Give me your money," he demanded.
Indignant, the affluent man replied,
"You can't do this—I'm a U.S. Congressman!"
"In that case," replied the robber,
"give me MY money!"

APRIL 18

Why does a slight tax increase cost you two hundred dollars and a substantial tax cut save you thirty cents?

APRIL 19

My wife and daughter were just finishing
dinner when my wife said "I over ate."
My daughter (age 4) was not
to be out done, said "I over nine!"

APRIL 20

Men stumble over the truth from
time to time, but most pick themselves
up and hurry off as if nothing happened.

WINSTON CHURCHILL

*Get the facts at any price, and hold on tightly
to all the good sense you can get.*

PROVERBS 23:23 TLB

APRIL 21

When the Jones family moved into their new house, a visiting relative asked the little five-year-old how he liked the new place. "It's terrific," he said. "I have my own room, Mike has his own room, and Jamie has her own room. But poor Mom is still sleeping with Dad."

APRIL 22

I dialed one of those 900 numbers for free financial advice. They advised me not to dial 900 numbers.

APRIL 23

I was shopping in an arts and crafts store, where a friend of mine worked, for a gift for my niece. She had taken an interest in oil painting and I planned to purchase a beginner set of paints and brushes. My friend was at the cash register when I was checking out. I hadn't seen her for a few weeks and had started a diet in the meantime, having moderate success. She asked me if I had gotten thinner. I was thrilled that it showed already and replied that I had lost a few pounds. She rolled her eyes and said, "I meant paint thinner."

APRIL 24

If I can be of any help, you're
in more trouble than I thought.

APRIL 25

Doctors can be frustrating.
You wait a month-and-a-half
for an appointment, and he says,
"I wish you'd come to me sooner."

APRIL 26

Mechanic: I couldn't repair your brakes, so I made your horn louder.

We can't go into the streets without danger to our lives. Our end is near—our days are numbered. We are doomed.

LAMENTATIONS 4:18 TLB

APRIL 27

An usher was passing the collection plate at a large church wedding. One of those attending looked up, very puzzled. Without waiting for the question, the usher nodded his head and said, "I know it's unusual, but the father of the bride requested it."

APRIL 28

$Q.$ What is an activity performed by 40% of all people at a party?

$A.$ Snooping in your medicine cabinet.

APRIL 29

A balanced diet
is a cookie in each hand.

APRIL 30

Four old men were out golfing. "These hills are getting steeper as the years go by," one complained. "These fairways seem to be getting longer too," said one of the others. "The sand traps seem to be bigger than I remember them too," said the third senior.

After hearing enough from his senior buddies, the oldest and the wisest of the four of them at 87 years old, piped up and said, "Just be thankful we're still on the right side of the grass!"

MAY 1

Learn from the mistakes of others. You can't live long enough to make them all yourself.

MAY 2

Tact is the ability to describe
others as they see themselves.

ABRAHAM LINCOLN

Do to others as you would have them do to you.

LUKE 6:31 NRSV

MAY 3

I don't believe in temporary
insanity as a murder defense.
People kill people, unfortunately.
Temporary insanity is breaking into someone's
home and ironing all their clothes.

MAY 4

There are only two kinds of people
in the world—those who wake up in the
morning and say, "Good morning, Lord!"
and those who wake up in the morning and say,
"Good Lord, it's morning."

MAY 5

Loan applicant: "I would like to borrow
$2,000 please."
Bank officer: "Certainly, sir. Over how long?"
Loan applicant: "Three years, please."
Bank officer: "OK, sir. We can do $75
per month for 36 months. Is that OK?"
Loan applicant: "No, not at all.
I want it all at once!"

MAY 6

Do you think Adam ever said to Eve,
"Watch it! There are plenty more
ribs where you came from!"

MAY 7

The man passed out in a dead faint as he came out of his front door onto the porch. Someone called 911. When the paramedics arrived, they helped him regain consciousness and asked if he knew what caused him to faint.

"It was enough to make anybody faint," he said. "My son asked me for the keys to the garage, and instead of driving the car out, he came out with the lawn mower!"

MAY 8

W hy should you borrow money
from a pessimist?
Because he never expects to get it back.

BOB PHILLIPS

*Let no debt remain outstanding, except
the continuing debt to love one another.*

ROMANS 13:8 NIV

MAY 9

While walking along the sidewalk in front of his church, our minister heard the intoning of a prayer that made him stop in his tracks. Apparently, his five-year-old son and his playmates had found a dead robin. Feeling that proper burial should be performed, they had secured a small box and cotton batting, dug a hole and made ready for the disposal of the deceased.

The minister's son was chosen to say the appropriate prayers and with sonorous dignity intoned his version of what he thought his father always said: "Glory be unto the Faaaather. And unto the sonnn...and into the hole he gooooes."

MAY 10

Church blooper: Ladies, don't forget
the rummage sale. It's a chance to get rid of
those things not worth keeping around the
house. Don't forget your husbands.

MAY 11

Ask your child what he wants
for dinner only if he's buying.

MAY 12

Felix, my husband, was playing golf with our town's fire chief when he hit a ball into the rough. As Felix headed for the brush to find his ball, the chief warned him, "Be careful, the rattlesnakes are out." The chief explained that calls had been coming in all week requesting assistance with removing the snakes.

"You've got to be kidding," Felix replied in astonishment. "People actually call the fire department to help them with rattlesnakes? What do you say to them?"

"Well," said the chief, "the first thing I ask is, 'Is it on fire?'"

MAY 13

It is bad to suppress laughter. It goes back down and spreads to your hips.

FRED ALLEN

MAY 14

Is the glass half empty, half full,
or twice as large as it needs to be?

You revive my drooping head;
my cup brims with blessing.

PSALM 23:5 THE MESSAGE

MAY 15

When everything's coming your way,
you're in the wrong lane.

MAY 16

As long as there are tests,
there will be prayer in schools.

MAY 17

Tech support people like me spend our days on the phone with customers. Many like to chat while waiting for their computers to reboot. One man told me he'd been a long-haul truck driver. "I'd love to drive a big rig," I said, "but I'd worry about falling asleep at the wheel."

"Here's a tip to stay awake," he offered.
"Put a $100 bill in your left hand
and hold it out the window."

MAY 18

1 kilogram of falling figs;
1 Fig Newton.

MAY 19

One evening after dinner, a small boy asked his father, "Where's Mommy?"

"Mommy is at a Tupperware party."

This explanation satisfied the boy for only a moment. Puzzled, he asked, "What's a Tupperware party, Daddy?"

Figuring a simple answer was the best approach, the man said, "Well, son, at a Tupperware party, a bunch of ladies sit around and sell plastic bowls to each other."

The boy nodded, then burst out into laughter, and said, "Come on, Dad! What is it really?"

MAY 20

Father: When Abe Lincoln was your age, he was studying books by the light of the fireplace.
Son: When Lincoln was your age, he was President.

Discipline your son in his early years while there is hope.

PROVERBS 19:18 TLB

MAY 21

I like work. It fascinates me.
I can sit and look at it for hours.

JEROME K. JEROME

MAY 22

A salesman is driving down a country road when he sees a young kid in front of a barn. On the barn are 5 targets with arrows in the bulls eye of each target. Screeching to a stop he runs out to the kid amazed that this kid could shoot so well.

"Son," he says, "how did you hit all those bulls' eyes?"

"Well sir," the boy replied, "I take the arrow and lick my fingers like this, then I take my fingers and straiten the feathers like this, take aim with my hand against my cheek, let go and where ever the arrow hits, I draw a bulls' eye."

MAY 23

If everything seems to be going well,
you have obviously overlooked something.

MAY 24

Boys will be boys, and so will
a lot of middle-aged men.

F. M. HUBBARD

MAY 25

Children are natural mimics who
act like their parents, despite every
effort to teach them good manners.

MAY 26

A second grader came home from school and said to her mother, "Mom, guess what? We learned how to make babies today." The mother, more than a little surprised, asked fearfully, "That's interesting. How do you make babies?" "It's simple," replied the girl. "You just change 'y' to 'i' and add 'es'."

MAY 27

If you fall on your face, look around…you're probably in good company.

Two are better than one…for if they fall,
one will lift up the other.

ECCLESIASTES 4:9-10 NRSV

MAY 28

You know you're old if you can
remember when bacon, eggs
and sunshine were good for you.

MAY 29

If you look like your passport picture,
you probably need the trip.

MAY 30

Writing to a magazine that had published his obituary: I've just read that I am dead. Don't forget to delete me from your list of subscribers.

RUDYARD KIPLING

MAY 31

It's amazing that the amount of news
that happens in the world everyday always
just exactly fits the newspaper.

J<small>UNE</small> 1

A person who lives in a glass house should...
change clothes in the basement.

JUNE 2

$\int$ome days are a total waste of makeup.

Your beauty and splendor have everyone talking.

PSALM 145:5 THE MESSAGE

JUNE 3

Children: You spend the first 2 years of their life teaching them to walk and talk. Then you spend the next 16 years telling them to sit down and shut-up.

JUNE 4

Never lend your car to anyone
to whom you have given birth.

ERMA BOMBECK

JUNE 5

First pilot, "I heard you got a new position with Earhart Air. Don't they have kind of a lousy safety record?"

"I'll say," answered the second pilot. "Last week two of their flight simulators collided."

JUNE 6

Q. There are more collect calls on this day than any other day of the year?

A. Father's Day

JUNE 7

Church blooper: The pastor will preach his
farewell message, after which the choir will sing,
"Break Forth into Joy!"

JUNE 8

"I thought I told you to keep an eye on your cousin," the mother said. "Where is he?"
"Well," her son replied thoughtfully, "if he knows as much about canoeing as he thinks he does, he's out canoeing. If he knows as little as I think he does, he's out swimming."

JUNE 9

Father: My boy, when you grow up
I want you to be a gentleman.
Son: I don't want to be a gentleman,
Pop. I wanna be like you.

BOB PHILLIPS

JUNE 10

Although we were being married in New Hampshire, I wanted to add a touch of my home state, Kansas, to the wedding. My fiancee, explaining this to a friend, said that we were planning to have wheat rather than rice thrown after the ceremony.

Our friend thought for a moment. Then he said solemnly, "It's a good thing she's not from Idaho."

JUNE 11

The scientific theory I like best is that
the rings of Saturn are composed entirely
of lost airline baggage.

MARK RUSSELL

JUNE 12

"Armstrong," the boss bellowed, "I happen to know that the reason you didn't come to work yesterday was that you were out playing golf! What do you have to say for yourself?"
"That's a rotten lie!" Armstrong protested. "And I have the fish to prove it!"

JUNE 13

I like pigs. Dogs look up to us. Cats look down on us. Pigs treat us as equals.

WINSTON CHURCHILL

JUNE 14

I don't believe in temporary insanity as a murder defense. People kill people, unfortunately, Temporary insanity is breaking into someone's home and ironing all their clothes.

JUNE 15

It is extremely embarrassing to come to your senses and find out you haven't any.

What's this? Fools out shopping for wisdom! They wouldn't recognize it if they saw it.

PROVERBS 17:16 THE MESSAGE

JUNE 16

A father is a thing that growls when it feels good...and laughs very loud when it's scared half to death.

PAUL HARVEY

JUNE 17

When my three-year-old son opened the birthday gift from his grandmother and found a water pistol. He squealed with delight and headed for the nearest sink. I was not so pleased. I turned to Mom and said, "I'm surprised at you. Don't you remember how we used to drive you crazy with water guns?"

Mom smiled and then replied, "I remember."

JUNE 18

Whenever I feel blue,
I start breathing again.

J∪NE 19

Recently my husband and I were in that "waiting to board" time at the airport when the gate agent made an announcement. "Attention in the gate area. A hearing aide has been turned in. It was found on the floor in the men's room. If you've lost your hearing aide...and can hear this announcement, please come on up and claim it."

JUNE 20

I read recipes the same way I read science fiction. I get to the end and think, "Well, that's not going to happen."

JUNE 21

Everyone has his day and some
days last longer than others.

With the Lord a day is like a thousand years.

JUNE 22

Health nuts are going to feel stupid someday,
lying in hospitals dying of nothing.

JUNE 23

I was trying to get my freshman history class to understand how the native tribes must have felt when they first encountered the Spanish explorers. "How would you feel," I asked, "if someone showed up on your doorstep who looked very different, spoke a strange language, and wore unusual clothes? Wouldn't you be a bit scared?"

"Nah," one boy answered, "I'd just figure it was my sister's date."

JUNE 24

Middle age is when broadness of the mind
and narrowness of the waist change places.

JUNE 25

My daughter went to a local Mexican
drive-thru and ordered a taco.
She asked for "minimal lettuce."
"Sorry," the cashier said, "we only
have iceberg, will that do?"

J$_U$N$_E$ 26

A very dirty little fellow came in from playing in
the yard and asked his mother, "Who am I?"
Ready to play the game she said,
"I don't know! Who are you?"
"WOW!" cried the child. "Mrs. Johnson
was right! She said I was so dirty, my own
mother wouldn't recognize me!"

JUNE 27

Everyone makes mistakes. The trick is to make mistakes when nobody is looking.

Who makes a mistake and I do not feel his sadness?
Who falls without my longing to help him?

2 CORINTHIANS 11:29 TLB

JUNE 28

When weeding, the best way to make sure you are removing a weed and not a valuable plant is to pull on it. If it comes out of the ground easily, it was a valuable plant.

JUNE 29

Evening news is where they begin with "Good evening," and then proceed to tell you why it isn't.

JUNE 30

Church blooper: Potluck supper Sunday at 5:00 P.M.—prayer and medication to follow.

JULY 1

While making rounds, a doctor points out an X-ray to a group of medical students. "As you can see," she says, "the patient limps because his left fibula and tibia are radically arched. Michael, what would you do in a case like this?"

"Well," ponders the student, "I suppose I'd limp too."

JULY 2

Alexander Hamilton started the U.S. Treasury with nothing—and that was the closest our country has ever been to being even.

WILL ROGERS

JULY 3

I use not only all the brains I have,
but all I can borrow.

WOODROW WILSON

If you think you know it all, you're a fool for sure; real
survivors learn wisdom from others.

PROVERBS 28:26 THE MESSAGE

JULY 4

Mosquito: An insect that makes
you like flies better.

J~u~LY 5

A tour guide was showing a tourist around Washington, D. C. The guide pointed out the place where George Washington supposedly threw a dollar across the Potomac River.

"That's impossible," said the tourist. "No one could throw a coin that far!"

"You have to remember," answered the guide. "A dollar went a lot farther in those days."

JULY 6

It might look like I'm doing nothing,
but at the cellular level I'm really quite busy.

JULY 7

Why is it, "A penny for your thoughts," but, "you have to put your two cents in"?

STEVEN WRIGHT

JULY 8

A guy traveling through the western United States stopped at a small town and went into the general store. The road had been dusty and he needed a drink. He bought a soda and lit up a cigar, casually looking around the store. As he stood there sipping his drink, he quietly began blowing smoke rings. After he blew nine or ten smoke rings into the air, an angry American Indian stomped up to him and said, "Listen, buddy, one more remark like that and I'm going to punch you right in the face!"

JULY 9

I've gone to look for myself. If I should return before I get back, keep me here!

I have tried my best to find you—don't let me wander off from your instructions.

PSALM 119:10 TLB

JULY 10

Remember the ark was built by amateurs
and the Titanic was built by professionals.

MIKEY'S FUNNIES

JULY 11

A group of expectant fathers sat nervously in the hall. A nurse beckoned to one of them and said, "Congratulations, you have a son!" Another man dropped his magazine, jumped up and cried, "Hey, what's the idea? I got here two hours before he did!"

JULY 12

Can something be both new and improved?

JULY 13

After shopping at a busy store, another woman and I happened to leave at the same time, only to be faced with the daunting task of finding our cars in the crowded parking lot. Just then my car horn beeped, and I was able to locate my vehicle easily. "Wow," the woman said. "I sure could use a gadget like that to help me find my car."

"Actually," I replied, "that's my husband."

JULY 14

A newscaster interrupted scheduled programming to announce the outcome of a political election. "More on candidates at 10 P.M.," he said. My ten-year-old son looked at me in disbelief. "I didn't know they could call politicians 'morons' on national television!" he said.

July 15

Where there's a will, there are
five hundred relatives.

The rich can be sued for everything they have,
but the poor are free of such threats.

PROVERBS 13:8 THE MESSAGE

JULY 16

A boy was watching his father, a pastor,
write a sermon. "How do you know what
to say?" he asked.
"Why, God tells me."
"Oh, then why do you keep crossing things out?"

JULY 17

A wife, one evening, drew her husband's attention to the young couple next door and said, "Do you see those two? How devoted they are? He kisses his young bride every time they meet. Why don't you do that?"

"I would love to," replied the husband, "but I don't know her well enough."

JULY 18

Living with a saint is more
grueling than being one.

ROBERT NEVILLE

JULY 19

When my husband and I arrived at an automobile dealership to pick up our car, we were told the keys had been locked in it. We went to the service department and found a mechanic working feverishly to unlock the driver's side door. As I watched from the passenger side, I instinctively tried the door handle and discovered that it was unlocked. "Hey," I announced to the technician, "it's open!" To which he replied, "I know—I already got that side."

JULY 20

Things may come to those who wait,
but only the things left by those who hustle.

J_ULY $2$1

Before you criticize someone,
you should walk a mile in their shoes.
That way, when you criticize them,
you're a mile away and you have their shoes.

*I looked for sympathy, but there was none,
for comforters, but I found none.*

JULY 22

You know you've had too much coffee
when your eyes stay open when you sneeze.

JULY 23

While I was visiting my sister one evening,
I took out a candy dispenser that was
shaped like a miniature person.
"How does that thing work?" she asked.
As I turned the figurine's arm to pop candy out,
my sister laughed.
"I see...it's a lot like my husband," she said.
"You have to twist his arm to get
anything out of him too!"

JULY 24

$\mathbb{A}$ lie can be half way round the world before the truth has got its boots on.

JAMES CALLAGHAN

JULY 25

English is an odd language. There is no egg in the eggplant, no ham in the hamburger, and neither pine nor apple in the pineapple.

What is the opposite of joy?
"Sadness."
And the opposite of depression?
"Elation."
And how about the opposite of woe?
"I believe that would be giddy-up!"

JULY 27

I used to think I was indecisive,
but now I'm not so sure.

*We toss the coin, but it is the Lord
who controls the decision.*

PROVERBS 16:33 TLB

JULY 28

A fellow computer programmer asked for my help in putting new software into operation. At first, he handled most of the work. Eventually, though, he asked me to help with the last phase of the training. When I sat down with one woman and told her I would be showing her how to make changes to the files, she sighed with relief. "I'm so glad you're teaching me instead of him." Surprised, I said that my colleague was far more experienced than I was. "Yes," she said, "but I feel much more comfortable with you. I get nervous around really smart people."

JULY 29

An consultant is someone who
takes a subject you understand
and makes it sound confusing.

JULY 30

A man spoke frantically into the phone:
"My wife is pregnant and her contractions
are only two minutes apart!"
"Is this her first child?" the doctor asked.
"No, you idiot!" the man shouted.
"This is her husband!"

JULY 31

This week, all our office phones went dead. I went to a neighboring office to contact the telephone repair people. They promised to be out between 8:00 A.M. and 7:00 P.M. When I asked if they could give me a smaller time window, the pleasant gentleman asked, "Would you like us to call you before we come?"

AUGUST 1

Man is a peculiar creature.
He spends a fortune making
his home insect-proof and
air-conditioned, and then eats in the yard.

AUGUST 2

Children seldom misquote you.
In fact, they usually repeat word for
word what you shouldn't have said.

In everything he followed the example of his father.

2 KINGS 14:3 NIV

AUGUST 3

Always and never are two words you should always remember never to use.

WENDELL JOHNSON

AuGusT 4

The school of agriculture's dean of admissions was interviewing a prospective student, "Why have you chosen this career?" he asked. "I dream of making a million dollars in farming, like my father," the student replied. "Your father made a million dollars in farming?" echoed the dean much impressed. "No," replied the applicant. "But he always dreamed of it."

AUGUST 5

Last night, I lay in bed looking up
at the stars in the sky and thought to myself,
"Where the heck is the ceiling?"

AuGust 6

My wife invited some people to dinner. At the table, she turned to our six-year-old daughter and said, "Would you like to say the blessing?"

"I wouldn't know what to say," she replied.

"Just say what you hear Mommy say," my wife said. Our daughter bowed her head and said: "Dear Lord, why on earth did I invite all these people to dinner?"

AuGusT 7

I was driving with my three young children one warm summer evening when a woman in the convertible ahead of us stood up and waved. She was stark naked! As I was reeling from the shock, I heard my 5-year-old shout from the back seat, "Mom! That lady isn't wearing a seat belt!"

AUGUST 8

Church blooper: For those of you
who have children and don't know it,
we have a nursery downstairs.

*Not that the troubles should come as any
surprise to you. You've always known that
we're in for this kind of thing.*

1 Thessalonians 3:3 the message

August 9

As I was driving home from work one day, I stopped to watch a local Little League baseball game that was being played in a park near my home. As I sat down behind the bench on the first-base line, I asked one of the boys what the score was.

"We're behind 14 to nothing," he answered with a smile on his face.

"Really," I said. "I have to say you don't look very discouraged."

"Discouraged?" the boy asked with a puzzled look. "Why should we be discouraged? We haven't been up to bat yet."

August 10

Anyone who says "Easy as taking candy
from a baby" has never tried it.

AUGUST 11

After my husband and I had a huge argument,
we ended up not
talking to each other for days. Finally,
on the third day, he asked where
one of his shirts was.
"Oh," I said, "So now you're speaking to me."
He looked confused, "What are
you talking about?"
"Haven't you noticed I haven't spoken
to you for three days?" I challenged.
"No," he said, "I just thought
we were getting along."

AUGUST 12

I read yesterday that a lot of grandfathers have
false teeth and use them to entertain their
grandchildren. I've stopped flossing.
I want to be a great grandpa.

KEN DAVIS

AUGUST 13

TEAMWORK...means never having
to take all the blame yourself.

AuGuSt 14

A guy was telling his friend that he and his wife
had a serious argument the night before.
"But it ended," he said, "when she came
crawling to me on her hands and knees."
"What did she say?" asked the friend.
The husband replied, "She said, 'Come
out from under that bed, you coward!'"

May you rejoice in the wife of your youth....
May you ever be captivated by her love.

PROVERBS 5:18-19 NIV

AUGUST 15

The trouble with being punctual is that
nobody's there to appreciate it.

FRANKLIN P. JONES

AUGUST 16

It was very crowded at the supermarket, and the customer in front of me had a large order. As the harried-looking clerk lifted the final bag for her, its bottom gave way, sending the contents crashing to the floor. "They just don't make these bags like they used to," the clerk blurted to the customer. "That was supposed to happen in your driveway!"

AUGUST 17

One of the most successful inventors of all time was the man who invented the hay-bailing machine. Needless to say, he made a bundle.

AuGuST 18

The guy from Montana was bragging about how large his cattle ranch was, saying, "It takes all day to ride out to the west fence, two days to reach the south fence, another day to get to my east fence, and two more days to get home." The Texan, chewing calmly on a piece of straw drawled, "Yeah, I had a horse like that once."

AUGUST 19

A camel is a horse designed by a committee.

ALEC ISSIGONIS

AUGUST 20

Why is it that when you're driving and looking for an address, you turn down the volume on the radio?

I will not listen to your music,
no matter how lovely it is.

Amos 5:23 TLB

August 21

Lettin' the cat outta the bag is
a whole lot easier than puttin' it back in.

AUGUST 22

A young mother overheard her 5-year-old granddaughter playing "wedding." The wedding vows went like this: "You have the right to remain silent, anything you say may be held against you, you have the right to have an attorney present. You may kiss the bride."

AUGUST 23

Laugh and the world laughs with you.
Snore and you sleep alone.

ANTHONY BURGESS

AUGUST 24

The new pastor was visiting in the homes of his parishioners. At one house it seemed obvious that someone was at home, but no answer came to his repeated knocks at the door. He took out a card, wrote "Revelation 3:20" on the back and stuck it in the door. When the offering was processed the following Sunday, he saw that his card had been returned. Added to it was this message, "Genesis 3:10." Checking his Bible to make sure he remembered the citation correctly, he broke up in gales of laughter. Revelation 3:20 begins "Behold, I stand at the door and knock." Genesis 3:10 reads, "I heard your voice in the garden and I was afraid for I was naked."

On the first day of school, a first grader handed his teacher a note from his mother. The note read, "The opinions expressed by this child are not necessarily those of his parents."

AUGUST 26

Warning: Dates in calendar are closer than they appear.

Surely you have a wonderful future ahead of you.
There is hope for you yet!

PROVERBS 23:17 TLB

AUGUST 27

For their anniversary, a couple went out for a romantic dinner. Their teenage daughters said they would fix a dessert and leave it waiting. When they got home, they saw that the dining room table was beautifully set with china, crystal and candles, and there was a note that read: "Your dessert is in the refrigerator. We are staying with friends, so go ahead and do something we wouldn't do!" "I suppose," the husband responded, "we could clean the house."

AuGust 28

$\mathbb{A}$ vacationer called a seaside hotel to ask
its location. "It's only a stone's throw
from the beach," he was told.
"But how will I recognize it?" asked the man.
Came the reply: "It's the one with all
the broken windows."

AuGust 29

The brain is a wonderful organ.
It starts working the moment you get
up in the morning and does not
stop until you get into the office.

ROBERT FROST

AuGust 30

As he was walking along the street
the minister saw a little girl trying to reach
a high doorknocker. Anxious to help,
he went over to her. "Let me do it, dear,"
he said, rapping the knocker vigorously.
"Great," said the little girl. "Now run!"

AUGUST 31

Living on earth is expensive but it does include a free trip around the sun every year.

SEPTEMBER 1

If you have nothing good to say about anyone,
come and sit by me.

ALICE LONGWORTH ROOSEVELT

Don't tell your secrets to a gossip unless you want
them broadcast to the world.

PROVERBS 16:28 TLB

SEPTEMBER 2

Silence is golden, and example is the best
teacher, so is a silent example a golden
teacher...or is a silent teacher a golden example?

SEPTEMBER 3

While visiting a friend who was in the hospital, I noticed several pretty nurses, each of whom was wearing a pin designed to look like an apple. I asked one nurse what the pin signified.

"Nothing," she said with a smile.

"It's just to keep the doctors away."

SEPTEMBER 4

Never argue with a stupid person.
First they'll drag you down to their level,
then they'll beat you with experience.

SEPTEMBER 5

I did my nurse's training at a hospital in Liverpool, England. My fellow students and I had little money for meals, so we ate the awful food provided at the hospital complex. Sometimes kindly visitors would give us some of the treats they had brought for patients who had not wanted to eat them. One night a woman brought a pie to the kitchen and said to me, "Would you eat this up, love?" Another student and I devoured every delicious crumb! Soon our benefactor returned, however, and asked, "Is me 'usband's pie 'ot yet, dearie?"

SEPTEMBER 6

Camping isn't what it used to be. "Honey,
I'm going to go get some firewood,
do you have change for a twenty?"

NICK ARNETTE

SEPTEMBER 7

Common-looking people are the best
in the world: that is the reason
the Lord makes so many of them.

ABRAHAM LINCOLN

*The Lord does not look at the things man
looks at. Man looks at the outward appearance,
but the Lord looks at the heart.*

1 SAMUEL 16:7 NIV

SEPTEMBER 8

Two young men applied for the same position. They had the same qualifications. In order to determine which to hire, the applicants were asked to take a test. Both men missed only one of the questions. The manager said to the first applicant, "Thank you for your interest, but we've decided to give the job to the other applicant." "But why? We both got 9 questions correct," asked the rejected applicant. "We have based our decision not on the correct answers, but on the question you missed," said the manager. "Your fellow applicant put down for question #5, 'I don't know the answer.' And you put down, 'Neither do I.'"

SEPTEMBER 9

A wise schoolteacher sends this note to all parents on the first day of school: "If you promise not to believe everything your child says happens at school, I'll promise not to believe everything he says happens at home."

SEPTEMBER 10

You have to marvel at the unique lunacy
of a language where a house can burn up as
it burns down,
and in which you fill in a form
by filling it out.

A high school senior saw an inspirational advertisement on television about becoming a teacher. She called the number shown: 1-800-2TEACH. After a woman answered, the student babbled on about how she thought she had found her life's calling and could she send her some information. The lady who answered the phone asked the student what number she was calling. The student told her. There was a pause. Then she said, "You misspelled TEACH."

SEPTEMBER 12

It is better to have loafed and lost
than never to have loafed at all.

JAMES THURBER

SEPTEMBER 13

I don't suffer from stress. I'm a carrier.

He's got some dirty, deadly disease.
The doctors have given up on him.

PSALM 41:8 THE MESSAGE

SEPTEMBER 14

After a quarrel, a husband said to his wife, "You know, I was a fool when I married you." She replied, "Yes, dear, but I was in love and didn't notice."

SEPTEMBER 15

While working as an airline customer-service agent, I got a call from a woman who wanted to know if she could take her dog on board. I told her the dog was welcome, as long as she paid a $50 charge and provided her own kennel. I further explained that the kennel needed to be large enough for the dog to stand up, sit down, turn around and roll over.

"I'll never be able to teach him all that by tomorrow!" the customer complained.

SEPTEMBER 16

Every day more money is printed
for Monopoly than the U.S. Treasury.

SEPTEMBER 17

First woman: My dog is so smart.
Every morning he waits for a paperboy
to come around and then he takes
a newspaper and brings it to me.
Second woman: I know.
First one: How do you know?
Second one: My dog told me.

SEPTEMBER 18

Once over the hill, you pick up speed.

SEPTEMBER 19

A common mistake people make when trying to design something completely foolproof is to underestimate the ingenuity of complete fools.

The wise accumulate wisdom;
fools get stupider by the day.

PROVERBS 14:24 THE MESSAGE

SEPTEMBER 20

After directory assistance gave me my boyfriend's new telephone number, I dialed him— and got a woman. "Is Mike there?" I asked.

"He's in the shower," she responded.

"Please tell him his girlfriend called," I said and hung up.

When he didn't return the call, I dialed again. This time a man answered.

"This is Mike," he said.

"You're not my boyfriend!" I exclaimed.

"I know," he replied. "That's what I've been trying to tell my wife for the past half-hour."

READER'S DIGEST

SEPTEMBER 21

Women's clothes: never wear
anything that panics the cat.

P. J. O'ROURKE

SEPTEMBER 22

Dentist: "Try to relax. I'll pull that aching
tooth in five minutes."
Patient: "How much will this cost?"
Dentist: "It'll be $100."
Patient: "That much for just five minutes work?"
Dentist: "Well if you prefer, I can pull
it out very slowly."

SEPTEMBER 23

A computer once beat me at chess,
but it was no match for me at kick boxing.

EMO PHILIPS

SEPTEMBER 24

One afternoon, a woman was in her back yard when a tired-looking dog wandered into the yard. The woman could tell from the dog's collar and well-fed belly that he had a home. When she walked into the house, the dog followed her, sauntered down the hall, and fell asleep in a corner. An hour later, he went to the door, and the woman let him out.

The next day the dog was back. He resumed his position in the hallway and slept for an hour. This continued for several weeks. Curious, the woman finally pinned a note to his collar: "Every afternoon, your dog comes to my house for a nap."

The next day he arrived with a different note pinned to his collar: "We have six children. He's trying to catch up on his sleep."

September 25

I am better than I was, but not quite
so good as I was before I got worse.

*You know that the testing of your
faith develops perseverance.*

JAMES 1:3 NIV

SEPTEMBER 26

A guy took his girlfriend to a football game for the first time. After the game he asked his girlfriend how she liked the game.

"Oh, I really liked it," she said, "but I just couldn't understand why they were killing each other for 25 cents."

"What on earth do you mean???"

"Well, I saw them flip a coin and one team got it and then for the rest of the game all they kept screaming was, 'Get the quarter back! Get the quarter back!'"

SEPTEMBER 27

Everyone is entitled to be stupid,
but some people abuse the privilege.

SEPTEMBER 28

"Here's something that will really make you feel grown up," said a father to his teenage daughter, "Your very own phone bill."

SEPTEMBER 29

There was a woman from Big Ugly,
West Virginia, who entered a beauty pageant,
and won. The next day the headline
in the local paper read, "Big Ugly Woman
Wins Beauty Pageant".

SEPTEMBER 30

$\mathbb{A}$ little child in church for the first time watched as the ushers passed the offering plates. When they neared the pew where he sat, the youngster piped up, "Don't pay for me, Daddy, I'm under five."

OCTOBER 1

A child's greatest period of growth
is the month after you've purchased
new school clothes.

I love you and want you to grow up well, not spoiled.

1 CORINTHIANS 4:14 THE MESSAGE

OCTOBER 2

Pat: Whenever I'm down in the dumps,
     I get myself another hat.
Sue: I wondered where you found them.

OCTOBER 3

As a traffic safety consultant, I often gave
talks on accident prevention. One night after
I spoke to a PTA group, the program
chairperson thanked me profusely
and gave me a check for fifty dollars.
"Giving these presentations is a part of my job,"
I said. "Could I donate the money
to one of your causes?"
"That would be wonderful!" she gushed.
"We have just the program that could use it.
We're trying to raise money so we
can afford better speakers."

OCTOBER 4

A hillbilly was making his first visit to a hospital where his teenage son was about to have an operation. Watching the doctor's every move, he asked, "What's that?" The doctor explained, "This is an anesthetic. After he gets this he won't know a thing." "Save your time, Doc," exclaimed the man. "He don't know nothing now."

OCTOBER 5

Always buy good shoes, and a good bed.
Because if you aren't in one, you're in the other.

OCTOBER 6

Some teachers at state universities get
to know our students fairly well.
One instructor told his communications
class of his plans to propose marriage.
A student spoke up and said that he had recently
asked his girlfriend to marry him as well.
"What was her answer?" the instructor asked.
"I don't know," the student replied.
"She hasn't E-mailed me back yet."

OCTOBER 7

You can't turn back the clock,
but you can wind it up again.

His mercies...are new every morning.

LAMENTATIONS 3:22–23 NRSV

OCTOBER 8

A little boy got lost at the YMCA and found himself in the women's locker room. When he was spotted, the room burst into shrieks, with ladies grabbing towels and running for cover. The little boy watched in amazement and then asked, "What's the matter—haven't you ever seen a little boy before?"

OCTOBER 9

I love deadlines. I especially like the whooshing
sound they make as they go flying by.

OCTOBER 10

Some people ask the secret of our long marriage. We take time to go to a restaurant two times a week. A little candlelight, dinner, soft music and dancing.
She goes Tuesdays, I go Fridays.

HENNY YOUNGMAN

OCTOBER 11

Accept that some days you're the pigeon
and some days you're the statue.

OCTOBER 12

I can't cook, hate to clean, and loathe ironing.
The only thing domestic about me is that
I was born in this country.

PHYLLIS DILLER

OCTOBER 13

W hen the going gets tough, the tough get going. The not-so-tough scream for help.

Pray every way you know how.

I TIMOTHY 2:1 THE MESSAGE

OCTOBER 14

My husband is wonderful with our baby daughter, but often he turns to me to tell him what to do. Recently, I was in the shower when he poked his head in to ask,

"What should I feed Lily for lunch?"

"That's up to you," I replied. "There's all kinds of food. Why don't you pretend I'm not at home?"

A few minutes later, my cell phone rang. I answered it to hear my husband asking,

"Yeah, hi, Honey. Uh…what should I feed Lily for lunch?"

OCTOBER 15

The HR representative asked me to fill
out a job application. One of the questions was:
Who should be notified in case of emergency.
I wrote: "A good doctor!"

OCTOBER 16

My son, 4, came screaming out of the bathroom to tell me he'd dropped his toothbrush in the toilet. So I fished it out and threw it in the garbage. He stood there thinking for a moment, then ran to my bathroom and came out with my toothbrush. He held it up and said with a charming little smile, "We better throw this one out too then, 'cause it fell in the toilet a few days ago."

OCTOBER 17

"This is the worst essay it has ever been my misfortune to read," ranted the teacher. "It has too many mistakes. I can't understand how one person would have made all these mistakes."

"One person didn't," replied Little Jackie defensively. "My father helped me."

OCTOBER 18

While I was preaching in a church in Mississippi, the pastor announced that their prison quartet would be singing the following evening. I wasn't aware there was a prison in the vicinity and I looked forward to hearing them.

The next evening, I was puzzled when four members of the church approached the stage.

Then the pastor introduced them.

"This is our prison quartet," he said, "behind a few bars and always looking for the key."

OCTOBER 19

A reporter was interviewing a 104 year-old woman: "And what do you think is the best thing about being 104?" She simply replied, "No peer pressure."

I've become wiser than the wise old sages.

PSALM 119:100 THE MESSAGE

OCTOBER 20

When I'm not in my right mind,
my left mind gets pretty crowded.

OCTOBER 21

One day a State Trooper was pulling off the expressway. When he turned onto the street at the end of the ramp, he noticed someone at a chicken place getting into his car. The driver placed the bucket of chicken on top of his car, got in and drove off with the bucket still on top of his car. So the trooper decides to pull him over and perform a community service by giving the driver his chicken. So he pulled him over, walked up to the car, pulled the bucket off the roof and offered it to the driver. The driver looks at the trooper and says, "No thanks, I just bought some."

OCTOBER '22

Church blooper: The eighth-graders will be presenting Shakespeare's Hamlet in the church basement on Friday at 7 P.M. The congregation is invited to attend this tragedy.

OCTOBER 23

If the English language made any sense,
lackadaisical would have something to
do with a shortage of flowers.

DOUG LARSON

OCTOBER '24

Cleaning your house while your kids are still growing is like shoveling the drive before it has stopped snowing.

OCTOBER 25

Retirement means twice as much
husband and half as much money.

OCTOBER 26

Nothing ventured, nothing gained—but if
everything is ventured, and still nothing gained,
give up and venture elsewhere.

PETER WASTHOLM

*The Lord will keep you from all harm...the Lord
will watch over your coming and going
both now and forevermore.*

PSALM 121:7-8 NIV

OCTOBER 27

A man in a hurry taking his 8-year-old son to school, made a turn at a red light where it was prohibited. "Uh-oh, I think I just made an illegal turn!" the man said. "It's okay, Dad" the boy said. "The police car right behind us did the same thing."

OCTOBER 28

Live so that you wouldn't be ashamed
to sell the family parrot to the town gossip.

WILL ROGERS

OCTOBER 29

A woman was trying hard to get the catsup to come out of the bottle. During her struggle the phone rang so she asked her four-year-old daughter to answer the phone. "It's the minister, Mommy," the child said to her mother. Then she spoke into the phone, "Mommy can't come to the phone right now. She's hitting the bottle."

OCTOBER 30

A tourist is picked up by a cabbie on a dark night. The passenger taps the driver on the shoulder to ask a question. The driver screams, loses control of the car, nearly hits a bus, drives up on the sidewalk, and stops inches from a shop window. For a second everything went quiet in the cab, then the driver said, "Look friend, don't EVER do that again. You scared the daylights out of me!"

The passenger apologizes and says he didn't realize that a "little tap" could scare him so much. The driver, after gathering himself together replied, "Sorry, it's not really your fault. Today is my first day as a cab driver—I've been driving hearses for the last 25 years!"

OCTOBER 31

Two peanuts were walking through a tough neighborhood. One of them was a-salted.

NOVEMBER 1

I think if I have a good breakfast I could
go without food for the rest of the day.
I think that until about lunchtime.

I eat my fill of prime rib and gravy, I smack my lips.
It's time to shout praises!

PSALM 63:5 THE MESSAGE

NoVember 2

We sometimes take English for granted,
But if we examine its paradoxes we find that:
Quicksand takes you down slowly,
Boxing rings are square,
And a guinea pig is neither from Guinea
nor is it a pig.

NOVEMBER 3

My friend's husband always teases
her about her lack of interest in household
chores. One day he came home with a gag gift,
a refrigerator magnet that read:
"Martha Stewart doesn't live here."
The next day he came home to find the magnet
holding up a slip of paper. The note read:
"Neither does Bob Villa."

NOVEMBER 4

Happiness is having a large, loving,
caring, close-knit family...
in another city.

GEORGE BURNS

NOVEMBER 5

Two wrongs don't make a right, but two Wrights did make an airplane.

NOVEMBER 6

A little boy opened the big and old family Bible with fascination, he looked at the old pages as he turned them. Then something fell out of the Bible and he picked it up and looked at it closely. It was an old leaf from a tree that had been pressed in between the pages. "Mommy, look what I found," the boy called out.

"What have you got there, dear?" his mother asked.

With astonishment in his voice he answered: "It's Adam's clothes!!!"

NOVEMBER 7

Keep the kitchen clean—eat out.

NOVEMBER 8

The congregation of a small church wanted to give a special thank you to their pastor for his fifteen years of ministry with them. At the end of the morning service, they presented the pastor and his wife with a trip to the Holy Land. The pastor said some special words and finished with "I thank you from the bottom of my heart."

His wife said some words and finished the same way. Not to be left out of all the celebration and speeches, their eight-year-old got up and said, "I thank you from my bottom also."

NOVEMBER 9

Early morning cheerfulness can
be extremely obnoxious.

WILLIAM FEATHER

When others are happy, be happy with them.

ROMANS 12:15 TLB

NOVEMBER 10

When I was visiting a friend who lived on the edge of a wilderness preserve, we drove along a rutted trail, and we saw a small creek ahead whose bridge was under water. "We have a serious beaver problem," our friend said. "They build dams that cause the creek to flood. Forest rangers take down the dams, and the beavers rebuild them." As we got closer, we could see a large scoreboard posted by the bridge. It read: BEAVERS 3, RANGERS 0.

NOVEMBER 11

I hate it when my foot falls asleep
during the day because that means
it's going to be up all night.

STEVEN WRIGHT

NOVEMBER 12

A lady went to the butcher shop looking for a chicken for dinner. She asked the butcher to see the selection. He only had one chicken left but did not disclose this to the lady. He kept the chickens in the bin below the showcase and so he reached down and pulled out his last chicken. He put it on the scale. The lady eyed the weight and asked if he had one a little larger.

"Yes," he replied. He took the chicken and lowered it down to the empty bin, shook it against the side and brought it back out. This time when he placed it on the scale his trained thumb hung just a little bit on the edge of the scale. The lady eyed the weight and said, "That is fine, I'll take both of them."

NOVEMBER 13

Don't let people drive you crazy
when it's within walking distance.

NOVEMBER 14

"So tell me, Mrs. Smith," asked the interviewer, "have you any other skills you think might be worth mentioning?"

"Actually, yes," said the applicant modestly. "Last year I had two short stories published in national magazines, and I finished my novel."

"Very impressive," he commented, "but I was thinking of skills you could apply during office hours."

Mrs. Smith explained brightly, "Oh, that was during office hours."

NOVEMBER 15

You know you're getting old when
the candles cost more than the cake.

BOB HOPE

There will come a time when your limbs will tremble
with age, your strong legs will become weak, and your
teeth will be too few to do their work, and there will
be blindness too.

ECCLESIASTES 12:3 TLB

NOVEMBER 16

Church blooper: While Pastor is on vacation, massages can be given to the church secretary.

NOVEMBER 17

My boyfriend and I were lunching
at a sidewalk café. Our waitress looked like
a real surfer girl: athletic with a great tan and
blonde hair. Mulling over the menu, my boyfriend
asked her if the roast beef was rare.
The waitress gave us a funny stare and replied,
"Well, no. We have it, like, just about every day."

NOVEMBER 18

Age is a question of mind over matter.
If you don't mind, it doesn't matter.

Satchel Paige

November 19

While working for an organization that delivers lunches to elderly shut-ins, I used to take my four-year-old daughter on my afternoon rounds. She was unfailingly intrigued by the various appliances of old age, particularly the canes, walkers and wheelchairs. One day I found her staring at a pair of false teeth soaking in a glass. As I braced myself for the inevitable barrage of questions, she merely turned and whispered, "The tooth fairy will never believe this!"

NOVEMBER 20

A man attempting to set up his new printer called the tech support number, complaining about the error message: "Can't find the printer." On the phone, the man said he even held the printer up in front of the screen, but the computer still couldn't find it!

NOVEMBER 21

A simple thank you will do. But a big thank you with a box of chocolates would do better.

I'm about to burst with song; I can't keep quiet about you. God, my God, I can't thank you enough.

PSALM 30:12 THE MESSAGE

NOVEMBER 22

At the company water cooler, I bragged about my children's world travels: one son was teaching in Bolivia, another was working in southern Italy, and my daughter was completing a year-long research project in India. One co-worker's quip, however, stopped me short. "What is it about you," she asked, "that makes your kids want to get so far away?"

NOVEMBER 23

By the time you can make ends meet,
they move the ends.

NOVEMBER 24

A priest and pastor from the local parishes are standing by the side of the road holding up a sign that reads, "The End is near! Turn yourself around now before it's too late!" They planned to hold up the sign to each passing car. "Leave us alone you religious nuts!" yelled the first driver as he sped by. From around the curve they heard screeching tires and a big splash. "Do you think," said one clergy to the other, "we should just put up a sign that says 'Bridge Out' instead?"

NOVEMBER 25

Madness takes its toll.
Please have exact change.

NOVEMBER 26

I was having lunch with my nine-year-old son, when the waitress came by to ask if we wanted a drink. "I'll have a decapitated coffee," my son said in all seriousness. The waitress smiled and poured him a cup. Not to be outdone, she returned with the coffeepot a few minutes later and said, "Can I put a head on that for you?"

NOVEMBER 27

$\mathcal{B}$eware of the half-truth. You may
have gotten hold of the wrong half.

*They are a nation of ninnies, they don't know
enough to come in out of the rain. If they
had any sense at all, they'd know this; they
would see what's coming down the road.*

DEUTERONOMY 32:28-29 THE MESSAGE

NOVEMBER 28

You know when you're sitting on a chair and you lean back so you're just on two legs then you lean too far and you almost fall over but at the last second you catch yourself? I feel like that all the time.

NOVEMBER 29

Good judgment comes from experience; and experience, well, that comes from bad judgment.

NOVEMBER 30

On her way back from the concession stand,
Sandra asked the man at the end of the row,
"Sir, did I step on your foot a minute ago?"
Expecting an apology the man said,
"Indeed you did."
Sandra nodded. "Oh, good.
Then this is my row."

DECEMBER 1

My sister was bemoaning the fact that she had procrastinated cleaning and organizing her house for a long time. Since she was planning to entertain, she felt a lot of pressure to get moving. That afternoon she phoned, sounding glum. "I went to the bookstore," she explained, "and I bought a book on how to get organized. I was all fired up, and decided to clean out all the shelves in the living room. While I was working, I found the same darn book. I had bought it a couple of years ago."

DECEMBER 2

Of course I don't look busy...I did
it right the first time.

DECEMBER 3

A jury consists of twelve persons chosen
to decide who has the better lawyer.

ROBERT FROST

DECEMBER 4

My friend wanted to learn to use the Internet but couldn't grasp virtual reality. She doesn't always grasp regular reality either.

Faith is being sure of what we hope for and certain of what we do not see.

HEBREWS 11:1 NIV

DECEMBER 5

We could learn a lot from crayons: some are sharp, some are pretty, some are dull, some have weird names, and all are different colors...but they all exist very nicely in the same box.

DECEMBER 6

If it weren't for caffeine I'd have
no personality whatsoever!

DECEMBER 7

Children will soon forget your presents.
They will always remember your presence.

DECEMBER 8

A lady was visiting a new church one Sunday. The sermon seemed to go on forever, and many in the congregation fell asleep.
After the service, to be social, she walked up to a very sleepy looking gentleman, extended her hand in greeting, and said, "Hello, I'm Gladys Dunn."
And the gentleman replied, "You're not the only one ma'am, I'm glad it's done too!!"

DECEMBER 9

It's dèjá vu all over again!

YOGI BERRA

DECEMBER 10

Happiness comes through doors
you didn't even know you left open.

*I have placed before you an open door
that no one can shut.*

REVELATIONS 3:8 NIV

DECEMBER 11

A bank is a place that will lend you money
if you can prove that you don't need it.

BOB HOPE

DECEMBER 12

A mother was showing her son how to zip up his coat. "The secret," she said, "is to get the left part of the zipper to fit in the other side before you try to zip it up." The boy looked at her quizzically: "Why does it have to be a secret?"

Eventually everything is going to be out in the open, and everyone will know how things really are.

MATTHEW 10:26 THE MESSAGE

DECEMBER 13

Birthdays are good for you; the more
you have, the longer you live.

DECEMBER 14

We were listening to a lecture on psychic phenomena in our Comparative Religions course. Our instructor told us about a woman who contacted police working on a missing-persons case. "She gave eerily detailed instructions on where to find the body," the teacher said. "In fact, the detectives did find the body just as she had described. Now what would you call that kind of person?"

While the rest of us pondered the question, a sheriff's officer taking the course raised his hand and replied, "A suspect."

DECEMBER 15

If it weren't for STRESS
I'd have no energy at all.

DECEMBER 16

Happiness is nothing more than good health and a bad memory.

ALBERT SCHWEITZER

Forgetting what is behind and straining toward what is ahead, I press on toward the goal.

PHILIPPIANS 3:13-14 NIV

DECEMBER 17

I bought my brother some gift-wrap
for Christmas. I took it to the gift-wrap
department and told them to wrap it,
but in a different print so he would know
when to stop unwrapping.

STEVEN WRIGHT

DECEMBER 18

Every ten seconds, somewhere on this earth,
there is a woman giving birth to a child.
She must be exhausted

DECEMBER 19

A woman went to the Post Office to buy
stamps for her Christmas cards.
"What denomination?" asked the clerk.
"Oh, good heavens! Have we come to this?"
said the woman. "Well, give me 50 Protestant
and 50 Catholic ones."

DECEMBER 20

A day without sunshine is like…night.

DECEMBER 21

In a never-ending effort to attract the unchurched, some churches have considered translating their unfamiliar terminology into familiar football phrases. One example: DRAFT CHOICE—the decision to sit near the front during the sermon to avoid the drafts in the back.

DECEMBER 22

Hospitality is making your guests feel at home—even when you wish they were.

DECEMBER 23

F or somehow, not only at Christmas,
but all the long year through, the joy that you
give to others is the joy that comes back to you.

JOHN GREENLEAF WHITTIER

DECEMBER 24

Behold, a virgin shall be with child, and shall bring forth a son, and they shall call his name Emmanuel…God with us.

MATTHEW 1:23 KJV

DECEMBER 25

Don't cry because it's over;
smile because it happened.

DECEMBER 26

The difference between genius and stupidity
is that genius has its limits.

DECEMBER 27

Jeff was taking the Christmas decorations out to the garage for another year's storage. His arms bull of boxes, he slipped, fell down the last two steps, and landed flat on the cold floor. His wife heard the noise and yelled, "What was that?"

"I just fell down the stairs," he explained.

She rushed into the garage, "Anything broken?!"

"No, no, I seem to be fine."

"No, I meant my decorations? Are any of them broken?"

DECEMBER 28

My house was clean last week.
Sorry you missed it.

DECEMBER 29

Learn from the past.
Live for today.
Look for tomorrow.
Take a nap this afternoon.

Are you tired? Worn out?... Come to me.... I'll show
you how to take a real rest.

MATTHEW 11:28 THE MESSAGE

DECEMBER 30

God put me on earth to accomplish a certain number of things. Right now I am so far behind, I will live forever.

DECEMBER 31